1

The Standards of Majesty

The Great High Angelic Emperor
Jahshua Christ Divine

Read other works by The Great High Angel

The Charm of Princes

Djinn Poems to Her Majesty

The Great High Championship of
The Great High Imperial Djinn
Volumes 1 & 2

The Legendary saga of Djinndom
Scenes 1-250 & 251-500

The Standards of Majesty

1st

God fall upon me with affection from your unending awesomeness
Show Thou God, Thine unlimited strength with generous pleasures
The magnitude of God is invincible & supreme, none can compare
This work is for God purely, to give thanks to God
Jahshua is saved by Jesus and gives glory to the Lord
The anointed art chosen and decidedly noble
Thus it is my duty to worship my Creator who has right reasons
Watch as God moves thine spirit with the hint of a whisper
See the grace of His Great High Imperial Majesty & Omnipotence
Jahshua is a scribe of The Almighty Lord, and a worker of miracles
The love and pampering of the most blessed overwhelms
 I shall forever be in the debt of God, He deserves my goodness
He deserves the best from all His creation, He is the most worthy
God, how You use my life is Your grace. I have surrendered to You
Lead me by Your love God, keep me from Your hot vexation
Make me always to walk perfectly to please You
God and appease Your wrath for my prayer is to go with You
Teach me Lord, I ask You for wisdom and grace and favor
I ask for the beauty to attract every eye and heart
God make me triumphant in my quest
Do not give up on God, God I will not give up on You
Please, Master, You are my Master, and I must ask mercy of You
or die a painful and vain life O Lord, rectify my good faith
Judge me by my faith and prayers Lord
Desire Thou to love me overgenerously and blessing abundantly
That is my prayer God, it is selfish but it is how I should glorify Thee
By the greatness I achieve in Thy name
Make mine legend the pinnacle of Zion
God make mine prayer before all others
And lead me rightly, and most righteously, by Thine Standard God

2nd

I shall always serve the Almighty Lord God, seeking His delight
God I demand Your favor, and I shall be accountable in the act
Lord, I am your son, make me Thine firstborn and love me only
Come to me God with lovely virgin belles and darlings in white
Find me God to lead me to the summit of Thine Holy Hill Zion
A Grand Imperial Palace Castle hath a master bed for Thee God
Reveal Thine secrets to me God upon it that my strength triumph
Upon Thine Majesty's bed O Father Ruler Magistrate Authority
Ye God art mine Keeper, and Owner, I kneel and prostrate to Thee
The heavens art dazzling, I am in awe at this very moment
For Thou The Lord God art a trillion infinities of wondrous bliss
When Ye call my heart is taken by sweet serenade
So I am at the mercy of Thine temptations, Yours my Lord
Pity me for I am wretched to my children
I sought always to be in Thine great good graces Majesty
Thy name is Jah, and Ye art my Father, Ye have anointed me
Therefore I am in debt of Thee Highest Hosanna, instruct me well
Ye have heard mine prayers, why do Ye torment me with trials Sire
Shall I also be cruel to be considered godly? I walk in Thine wake
I live by the light of Thine inspiration God and pray to satisfy Thee
The Lord hath made a rich man and a poor man, & loves them both
He hath made a saint and a sinner and enjoys them as He prefers
God have mercy upon me who seeks amazement and joy for Thee
The mind of the Lord is ever so vast and capable of daunting feats
I am in love, I am in awe, I am in fear of my Creator
He hints to me His wrath and I cower at the strokes of His anger
Lord, I have sown Thine seeds may mine harvest yield richly so
O be Thou pleased God, please, I am only Your play thing
I am a tool for Your use that You have crafted to suit You
O God I pray to be used for the purpose of glory and majesty

3rd

God The Noble Majesty who reigns supreme as the ultimate
Totalitarian God Commander of The Generals' Grand Emperor
He is Omnipotent unto the maximum capacity infinite above all
Throughout is Hosanna the Highest, He rules supreme by
His Holy Mighty Spirit that cannot be thwarted ever.
Ferocious is The Lord of The Heavens He accepteth no evil
This is God. A poem is in the tongue of Jahshua
God speaketh. He quoth. Be thou in love with mine Servant
He proclaimeth and explaineth his reasoning in a confidence
All other poets art is disastrous and separate from the spirit of Jah
Here is Jah pure in His majestic form. He ruleth the skies and the
Earth most sacred, Globe atop the pinnacle of a mountain
A poet who writes a book be worthy of majesty
In my library beside my diary across from mine dresser beheth
crown scepter cape coat my cruise ships & intergalactic empire.
Your goodness protects me God. Your blood is blessing me.
I pray Lord to be unto Thee blessed in comparison
You have knelt before me God, as a Father and bathed me
I am of a Holy Spirit His Name is The Lord Glory and Emmanuel
God speaketh, He quoth "Rise up mankind. Go unto the stars.
There shall Ye find a whole new wealth of commodities."
I agree with the Lord. Express His commands.
I will not be petty, nor vain. I will not be inconsiderate.
I shall not forsake my vows. I long to be innocent. Please.
Lord, make me to be a good servant for You. I need Your approval.
Grand justice God, glory for You, love divinity and sovereignty
Make me above Your standards Lord, for mine soul's satisfaction
Please God, for my eternal soul's satisfaction

4th

Listening for God, He hears prayers to Him, He answers
The Lord answers prayers Hallelujah! Thank God constantly
Evermore I am His pet, and His favorite. I want to brag Lord
I want to boast in You, please let me boast Lord, in You
Let me boast and sing good praises dedicated to Thee
In the free world I speak as a high emperor genii
I get what I want God fawns over me with his arms around
Give generously to me God. I am hungry to know your love.
My love letters to the Lord are priceless. Treasure them Sire.
None else shall I call Sire but the Son and The Holy Spirit
Yet I am ever and always the Immortal Father. The Keeper of Zion
God hath possessed me with His Spirit I am overcome.
Revelations cause revolutions let ours be for peace
Our revelation is majesty we support the cause of The Lord
Tell of His wisdom and comprehension, He answers us perfectly
Astounding Lord Thy love is amazing. Show it by Your favor God
Where I go I shall uphold Thee and Thine laws O God
Teach me to be perfect and most desirable and most wonderful
By Thine commands I strive to live Lord You are the only assurance
Make me ruler over all armies, Father to 10,000, and High Emperor
God how can I test the master, I only seek to know Your wisdom
God I seek to know the great pleasures of godliness
I am Thine apprentice learning to rule. I am Thine prince Lord
Thine Holy Empire is restored with the purity of Jahshua
Whose blood is washed by Emmanuel
The sacrifices of men art savage, enlighten us Lord
I came unto Thee for solace, and immediately I was content
Thank God for all of His mysteries, may He care for everyone
Lord, You are my Lord and I stand for Thee with faith
You are a firm stable foundation that holds me up

5th

God's thinking is sure and despises all evil and wickedness
His purity is perfect evil is the restlessness of His desire to be
Therefore His soul must settle within us in order to walk rightly
When the soul is settled peace is supreme and desire is petty
Be high in majesty God, Thine realm is Thine creation
Create genius Lord, Jahshua be Thine most cherished
His prayer be Thine own prayer, Omniscient Lord
Let me not suffer in longing God, and answer mine prayer
For the repute of Thine mercy, care, and compassion
shall be damaged severely by the pain of this Thine servant
Who only hoped to win Thine absolute favor
None have prayed as I have God, nor shall they ever
Ye heard me first of all the spirits and promise to answer me
O God, I trust Thee and am comforted to find this standard
My ghost is rich with potential far beyond the bohemians
More wealthy than the illuminati shall ever become
Mine commitment and faith art prepared for the death
And I shall no longer be with you, but you will be with me
Find me in obeisance God, I kneel & plead to Thee in earnest
Yea for the virginity of mine empress the queens and concubines
Must I die to go to heaven Lord? You the all capable
Could you love me enough while I glorify You?
While I give to Thee mine potential? Take Thine place in me
Be Thou in heaven with Jahshua my Lord
Would Ye speak to those adored to win me their respect & love
God promote Your Emperor keep Jahshua always in Your favor
In great grand wonderful castles palatial & stunning set Your Prince
Your son, his name is Jahshua, and he hath faith in the Lord
Reveal the truth of Your magnitude with generosity unto Jahshua
For he promotes and extols the Heavenly God of Hosts

6th

For Our Sons and Daughters, We shall be high royalty O Father
Here is to thy nobility O prince and to thine firstborns
God requireth of us nothing, but rewardeth us with love
How shalt the Lord love thee? Will He find thee praying?
Never leave mine ear God nary stop caring for me only
Lord am I selfish while You are mine cause, or am I faithful
I choose to be faithful, I will give Your love away to the blessed
Ye will provide mine provision from Thine infinite resource
Lord provide an abundance of delicious things & win mine empress
Sway her true love to me O Lord for a good wife she shall make
By Thine favor Ye have promised mine eternal soul mercy
God, cast me not into hell. I only want to be innocent
I want not the heat of Thine hot choler for Thine rage is furious
While the sky is black and deep the light of God is a gift
Time hath come to pass as the life of Jahshua, attend to him
Care for him with respect for high majesty and Holiness
A prophet is a guide upon the path of righteousness
But Jesus Christ Emmanuel is the way, the truth, and the life
We are in His heaven, I will wait for His return and live
Come to assure us O Savior by reasserting the desire of Our Lord
Never doubt the care of The Lord, keep faith in His testings
for His wisdom surpasses reality and reverses time
A doubt is a burden, but a prayer is a plea, pray for God's help
A life of devotion to God does not end, one should never quit faith
The life of a scribe is honorable Lord, build mine house with joy
I have sworn by Thy Name Jah, be Thou perfect for Thine prestige
God, miracles art a tremendous event, do not crush me please
For Thee Lord I stand with confidence having surrendered
God the days of bliss art best and Your love is splendid to behold
Give no power to the wicked one, that mine path be straight

7th

God is the unity of men and His laws art clear unto the upright.
Go to God for His guidance. He waits in broad & open daylight.
To rest in the comfort of His keep among the flock of the innocent
is a good situation, but to go forth in search of the lost is noble
We art not hunters, not cannibals, nor predators, we art humane
and humanity is benevolent for the honor of God's conscience
Our mercy and compassion art unto the Lord decent and beloved
Rejoice in the safety and protection of The Manifest Almighty
His genius is upon His pupil, His student shall be an apprentice
His pet will attend His state, and thus be Holy endowed
according to the standard of majesty beset by The High Emperor
Humility charity goodwill strength meekness kindness generosity
Love joy peace patience faith gentleness goodliness self restraint
These art the virtues of dignity which is worthy of respect
yea also according to the standard beset by His Foremost Majesty
The commandments of absolution art set for all time everywhere
All who know the laws of sanctity defend them unto the expanse
Thy neighbor shall come to thine aid, and God will stay with you
So long as ye as servants uphold and respect The Lord
The promise is on the life of the original spirit of prophecy
God is with us Emmanuel His Name is Jah He will prevail
Music is the language of heaven where poems art highly esteemed
An evil spirit sings a dissonant dirge and is loathed by the lofty
Lord Almighty make my song a pleasant and glorious hymnal
Purify mine essence and origin, wash me of all iniquity God
Inspire my hands with the loveliest anthems O to worship Thee
And that I be held in the highest regard by Thine judgement
and the judgement of every soul, I pray unto Thee Lord God
I pray unto Thee with conviction desperation & trusting hope
I have put mine prayers to Thee O Master, as Thine steward

8th

God surely hath these senses and that which stimulates them
The Lord should not be denied His delight which is mine servitude
Be it a pleasure to please the Lord who loves by His emperor
His majesty is set upon Jahshua as if a cape draped around him
Thick & towering neck over rugged shoulders with great strength
God is the all inspiring muse who revels in His every single work
The Great High Majesty is His most prized treasure and enterprise
Jahshua is the Supreme Champion of God, & the judgement is thus
The Lord & Savior Jesus Christ is The Way The Truth & The Life
There is no prophet above Him, Jesus, and His law is perfect
More perfect than Moses, Muhammad, David, or St. Paul,
Look to Jesus for thine wisdom, and strength, and so be fulfilled
For there is no king no prince no prophet endowed with perfection
Only the Lord Messiah Savior and King of Heaven, Jesus Christ
Is anointed with the purity of God, none but He is fit to rule Zion
Jahshua stands at the left of Jesus presenting Him
The right hand of the high emperor entitles the king of heaven
The other religions art cursed according to sacred laws
With Jesus at our head our race shall not tremble
Our station shall be inviolable under the law of Christ
The Great High Empire of God hath established to everyone
Its most Noble, most Holy, and most Sacred constitution
solely in the doctrine of the gospels of Jesus Christ
Faith is with God and is perfect under the authority of Christ
for love is always our motivation as it is peace to the soul
and love is the foundation of all of the work of Emmanuel
The love of God is providence but can only be attained through
the genuine admiration and respect of God Our Father
We must serve our Lord with the greatest humility and care
DREAD THE WRATH OF GOD! SHAME TO ALL US SINNERS!

9th

Jump up to an upbeat sound praising God's great goodness
The Lord is brightness and darkness shall be thwarted
The substance of light is energy while God is the fabric
God is therefore the force within the matter that hath life
The sensation of God comforts my nerve. May it come to you
Secure me Lord with Your helping hand guide me up Mt. Zion
In great castles among large pastures keep mine family safe
O Lord in sovereignty over the household, make me O Lord
For the undeniable majesty of Thy Name and empire
God with thine empire mine empress queens & concubines
make mine life a testimony of Thine loving generosity O Lord
Your poet scribe psalmist reveals the forecast of Your nature
The preference of God is nobility and decency as told by Christ
O to live in Your good graces carries me up high raising me
Look and see what God hath done for His flawless eminence
God I am in this moment thankful to be Your servant, be loved
Father as Your son I have grown for the labor at hand
Promote me to Thine favor and endow me with absolute supremacy
Over the entirety of Thine creation to give faith and hope to all
even to those who art high with thee, especially to the lowly
God set me at the tower top of an unsurpassable pinnacle
guarding mine fortress and keep with Thine omnipotence
Yea which is Thine and of Thyself, while I am to please Thee
Let us bring Thee joy Lord with love for Thy honor
O that this be a contract of Your humanity Lord
I uphold Your legacy God for Ye art worthy of posterity
Should our legends be braided forever bound in revolution
That majesty be unto Thee in every era forever
You are beautiful in every way God unparalleled
I live as Ye prefer I can only hope for Thine favor & blessing

10th

God is Master of karma and fortune, pay Him the highest regards
the disloyalty of rebels is a detriment to all subjects of Earth & Zion
There is but one God and one law which He protects called Christ
Praising the Lord is the best of habits. Thank God endlessly
Recite a standard of majesty to be thou remembered in goodness
It is right to give God our best. He hath infinite love to grant
To see the stars in the sky is to look upon the choirs of angels
Cherubs in a song play to seraphs dancing round them
The Holy spirit indeed hath an origin and it is the highness drops
Treasure the pleasure of the great emperor most grand of princes
The capitol of anarchy is the tower Jahshua The Great High Genii
His court is before him with his army behind and beneath him
The angels have set the king in His bed chambers to sleep awhile
His attendants await his orders in prayer for their high majesty
Forever live the prince of peace on Earth and in Heaven
My king I am the mighty djinn and I will keep your borders
I am the emperor of heaven and hell and you art mine firstborn
Mine prince in heaven, mine prince on earth, be they safe from hell
Salvation is an everlasting mercy from Our God all wonderful
This work is meant to honor the Lord for His loving charity
Love is unconditional, and favor is pleasant, love and favor me God
God mine prayers art solemn and sober and not done for vanity
fulfill mine behest God, or I shall be unto Thee a disappointment
Pray I do not disappoint my Lord. Pray He indulge mine potential
Standards art pointed for the cause of influence among nobles
Among savages one must be clever nimble wise and strong
From savagery arises nobility & from nobility harmony
From harmony peace then serenity then felicity toward bliss
In providence there is elation which enhances the experience
The excitement of adventure is magnified with elevated risk

11th

Do not hide Yourself from me God, for You art mine comforter
I need You for everything God, please stay and keep me well
without You God, without Your favor, there is only sorrow & pain
Lord be with me always and do not let me go, carry me God
I am afraid to fall down or to be led astray by wicked devices
Please do not make me afraid God, ease mine anxiety I plead
Eliminate mine discomforts and be Thine Self rewarded in it Lord
Let none disturb the peace of The Great High Emperor nor his joy
She prays for the stars and seeks the galaxies God answers her
Jahshua is the answer of the Lord, never doubt his wisdom
Pleasing Thee is what I live to do Jah, You my Father I Thy son
May the empire satisfy its treasured sovereign and His family
The wife of God is a wise empress and His children art His heirs
The kingdoms of mine empire art many, protected by arch angels
The hand of Hosanna crushes those who oppose His willing grace
Vile ones have violated the grace of God by their intentions
The goodly rely on God and shall not lose faith in Him
even in the most dire situation, in any moment God is all capable
Pray unto the Lord with faith and Ye shall be transported
Jah mocks us for our simplicity loving the babies and children
He The Lord I Am hath assurance with Jahshua and flaunts it
Is Jahshua foolish to trust in God?
He thinketh not in the unconditional devotion to His Name
I am a blessed being with endless potential for the Lord's repute
He shall make His reasons known in the appropriate time
This is by the wisdom of Our Creator who is Himself singular
Without Him the cosmos collapse in His anger the galaxies crumble
Help me to perform my task with perfection by Your instruction
Dwell in majesty God, always in a dignified and honorable state
Thine judgement is predominantly most fair, preeminent it is

12th

Thine cannot be overcome, cannot be thwarted Lord ever
The cause to please Thee is most glorious and noble
The beauty of Thine work enshrouds Zion even
Ye have set mine palace atop Zion with sumptuous stables
housing winged horses with golden tails hooves and manes
The skies above Thy Holy Hill withhold Thine infinite mystery
You have made mine chariot of bronze, or titanium
Mine vestments of cotton leather and silk art modest
Raise the mountain up under me and mine fortress Father
As I call up Your new borns from the peak of the pinnacle
Here confess I mine faith in He who is called The Lord God
I am prepared for Thine labor O Master Ye have employed me
My sons and daughters I leave within Thy care God
Promise me God Ye shall bless them forever from mine faith
I have sacrificed mine heart at Thine alter mine Maker
I cannot revoke my oath, let me not break it Lord
Give me victory in my quest and satisfaction in my life God
Your realm is limitless and mine prayer is simple to Thee
Though I am one with Thee the wretched contend against us
Why do Ye stand for my suffering God? I only do as Ye tell me.
Ye have made mine faith sacred forever unto all generations
Reward me justice for mine dedication to Thine satisfaction
My meditation is Thy contentment, and my prayer Thy favor
Ye have given me the opportunity to please Thee, so I shall
Take heed to the singularity of mine campaign which is Thine
Lord God, I have denied the world to answer Thy charge
Come to my defense while I represent Thy faithful O Lord
More might, more genius, more passion God than ever before
Supercharge me to the maximum power that Ye find new esteem
Ye have given Thyself license Lord to awe with miracles

13th

How should I ask Thine forgiveness Master? If it mean so much?
I shall print these standards to You God for a repentance of sin
I seek to be in Thy good graces and long for pardon for my fault
Never did I hope to disappoint Thee God, I love Your cause
It is unwise to go against the Lord, He is judging us constantly
Ye deserve more thanks than I can give; may all Your subjects rave
Of the love of the Liege Lord of Everything Jah the Almighty ruler
O Persuade every spirit to promote our cause God Your
satisfaction
God a good Father loves His sons, and doth not hate them
He loves them with all that he hath and favors him generously
Ye art the most generous Father, but Ye art still expanding
What can we expect of a God without limits and boundaries
Lord my soul hath one burning necessity which is mine empress
May our matrimony be forever bound with endless love
Assure me of Thine goodwill O Lord, it is what I hope for
Striving to serve Thee perfectly I have denied worldly things
and pray only for the sign of Your favor O Jehovah
Ye test mine prayers with trials to measure its yearning
While I waited on Thee God, Ye rebuked me with cruel scorn
The trauma of Your punishment baffles me with questions
Why should the all wise all merciful Lord be so horrid
Be mine hero O Lord, not a villain, not a rotten child
Swear to me God that Ye shall preserve me with gladness
And never to let down humanity, never quit us God
I have learned from my sins that they be not in vain
but I regret mine sinfulness for the shame it causes me
Renew me God, that I may prove mine true humility
There is only You to thank God, only You have power
Ye have caused me fault, that I know my place
God, I only seek peace and the sign of a grateful Lord

14th

The Lord is noble, is majestic and glorious with compassion
He is the Wonderful Father who loves His children with favors
God owes nothing but gives everything unto His committed
His love is assured to those who know Him intimately
We ask His secrets and the Lord shares with His cherished
I keep my God in confidence and He explains when I listen to Him
I stick close to Him as He leads us along scenic highways
His majesty set in His opulently lavish caravan
He and His princes upheld by angels that adore them
The emperor sits in His temple and commands the cosmos
The sky brushes His fortress as He peers through the windows
Existence surely resides in Jahshua. It is His pleasure
Come and kneel before God and He shall call forth His son
There is glory in Zion because of His majesty The Lord
The Creator of my life is amazing and terribly impressive
I am in the fear of God I am begging His great mercy
May the Lord be loved and fawned upon by His children
Treat the high princess as a fine and expensive treasure
Value the princes of great majesty above all things
Set them all in impenetrable shelters of Your wealthy empire
Guard Thine servant the high sheriff who keeps Your place
Yea God, may Your mercy be to answer my prayer
Which is the children of her majesty and Your emperor
Which is that their relations be protected forever
Their houses, their families, their offspring, protected always
God see to the glory of Your name which is Your empire
Never part our majesty God, never separate Your imperial heads
Favor Your devoted prince O Supreme Leader with adoration
Have compassion on Your son who exalts You Holy Father
Grand above all else with holding unlimited mysteries

15th

As with Jacob a revival of God's passion is with Jahshua
As with Abraham, Isaac, Joseph, and Israel, The Imperial Dynasty
Jahshua shall be father of many nations and people
The seed of the high majesty shall be vast & potent with goodness
A heathen hath no morals no statutes no code of ethics to abide by
They do not fear authority for they have no sense of it
The noble heed discipline and adhere to upright behavior
knowing what is good by wise discernment they choose rightness
Evil shall not extend past its own wicked humiliation
but the righteousness of the honorable shall be upheld forever
God the fire within me scorches but I shall endure with dignity
Mine outrage is vehement but I shall focus on probity
God my deliverer hath anointed me champion of decency
to discern what is right and just from what is abominable
The tyranny of evil men is an organization of hypocrisy
The illuminati is a network of despots that feed on the earth
like wolves they feed on the meek the simple and the peaceful
They have stolen our God given liberties for their treasuries
laying waste to the bounty of nature for the sake of worldly gain
but Jahshua shall teach them the meaning of love and unity
By his grace the high emperor shall show the rewards of mercy
For fear inspires rebellion, but love is the foundation of loyalty
an empire is invaluable and cannot be bought with capital
An emperor is an ally in a time of need whose justice is fair
He is not a dictator who reigns over his subjects by force
but heeds the voices of his denizens with compassionate humility
The people want comfort, repose, health, safety, and security
God shall provide it them under a universal empire of majesty
when they surrender their souls to the Holy sanctity of God
and leave off their selfish ambitions of egocentric vanity

16th

Under the order of God shall the nations be harmonious
There shall be no scruples among His stewards nor soldiers
Those wasteful and obsolete enterprises shall be dissolved
His majesty shall organize His empire to its maximum faculty
The corporations of the earth shall be dissolved in its unity
The hierarchy of high majesty shall be altruistic and fair
Its objective shall be peace and stability among its subjects
rather than the calamitous irresolution of dubious institutions
No governments nor conglomerates only one majestic hierarchy
The reign of the emperor is orderly and just for God is His will
The flock hath lost their way in pursuit of futile ventures
But God hath established His majesty with Jahshua for good
Recall the simplicity of servitude and how glorious it was
one leader one cause one objective and therefore one nation
Our children be taught nobility, love, and loyalty to one crown
and the preservation of honorable houses shall be assured
The dignity of patriots recognized and rewarded rightfully
One religion and one faith uniting all kingdoms forevermore
The majesty of God is set on utopia which is peace indeed
His emperor is designated to stand for one God embodied
The pilot of integrity, the navigator of union, the sign of truth
The degradation & degeneration of man hath come to its end
For Jahshua is purely noble by the edification of The Lord God
The immoral and iniquitous shall be brought low by ignominy
While the upright and virtuous shall be promoted to honor
Thus is majesty, thus is the justice of prudence and discipline
Far too long hath this people been ruled by vicious savagery
O ye wicked, are ye so astonished at this thine upheaval
when for so long the day of judgement hath been prophesied
Ye have fallen asleep O wretch, and shall be left in inferiority

17th

A family is not made wicked by the wealth of their estate
but by the poverty of the poor and the sickness of their servants
The separation between the rich and poor is increased by greed
and majesty is negated by the ostentatiousness of one's display
More beautiful than gold is compassion, than diamonds, charity
Opulence and luxury art not the same as majesty, for they art base
The highness of majesty is in its upright and honorable morality
There is an emperor and there is a tyrant, but they art not the same
The emperor seeks the love of his people and their happiness
While a tyrant only hath the heart to oppress and exploit his people
A house set upon a hill sends a cascade upon those below it
By its weight and size overcomes the structures surrounding
Yet the greatness of his manor will become burdensome to him
when he is alone with none to help him keep the seigniory
There is no fealty as dependable as love to a sovereign lord
The ruler who's people love him will fight more fiercely for him
than the ruler who's people fight for him out of fear of his rule
A title without which doth not increase is vain it shall be infamous
they who seize power for the sake of control art vacuous in that
for they will exchange their hardships for even greater toils
Power is not a gift, it is a responsibility which one is made for
comfort is a gift, peace is a gift, love is a gift, but rule is work
The king sits on his throne above a kingdom of scrutinizers
and shall teach his prince the ways of good conduct in authority
but blessed is the poor with simplicity, and the meek who is pitied
for they art satisfied with only a little and overjoyed by majesty
the excellency is where our blessedness is beheld in fact
Excellence that comes from the increase of bounty in life
This excellence is most excellent in the hands of the destitute
for the greatness of their appreciation exceeds the norm

18th

The high majesty is most excellent it surpasses all knowledge
God hath sent forth signs hourly, and even every minute
to announce his proclamation to every ear everywhere
The highest angel is also the greatest djinn for ruling both kingdoms
The return of the prince is to his princess: prepared in bridal attire
He is arrayed in the garb of the highest ranking offices of mankind
The prince walks with him the wisdom that he shares interests him
as the magnificence of existence is richness to the spirit
even more is the love of a people who have been well cared for
so the princess is a most precious treasure as she entices him
The Lord sets me to His task so that I have no alternative
thus I become a slave to His glory and shall live for His pleasure
What hath God given if He hath only given unto Himself?
The most generous Lord is greatly blessed by this His servant
for the suffering that I endure is to extol His delight
and all day God is in need of love and commitment
or else The Lord is regretful of His creation for He finds no joy in it
Serve God without ceasing that He find the desire to bless thee
Support universal peace. Support The Great High Empire.
God tells the answers to Jahshua, and Jahshua knows all things
for he is in the midst of God who lives as the high genii
You are for the joy of the Lord O ye who serve righteousness
the nobles art Christian and the dignified art upright in goodness
Here is a fundraiser for highness, blessedness, and happiness
One billion copies sold and Jahshua grants all favors
Come unto the high throne called Jahshua the imperial genii
and rally around his cause which is God's assumption of rule
Heed the command of His Majesty and be honored as grace
be accountable as excellence and dutiful as eminence
be thou knowledgeable as highness that the people be docile

19th

Her majesty's elegance is natural, emerging from her spirit
His majesty reaches out to her, it seeks out her affections
God hath blessed to be blessed and loved to be loved
He is worthy of love as He hath bestowed her beauty upon my eye
He hath set my sense in the warmth of her aura so I am indebted
to Him I am indebted for the sweetness of her scent
and I am His servant forever because He hath shown me her face
God Almighty I pray to Thee for Thine extreme and eternal love
and for the true love and favor of mine empress
O Lord I have asked as Ye have instructed that I would receive
I have come to Your door knocking that I would enter unto Thy help
O God, the state of thine steward is definitive of Thine goodness
Ye give generously and I am humbled to ask majesty of Thee
In the richest land I wish to thrive, that Ye would be renowned
As a sovereign of the law and lord of every entity to amuse my Lord
O yet the genii will never own the individual and untame spirit
She is in love with another, her majesty is. But I beg for her love
There is none who will love thee empress like thy great high angel
The heart of thy throne majesty is in excruciating pain
his immortal spirit sears in agony and cannot die
He cries in pain ever more wishing to touch thine hand
The love of his fellowship is dire to the emperor
he needs all people to love him and pray for him
he needs the faith of the congregation
Only the devil would stand against Jahshua
for the cause of the emperor is God's Holy will
and to love without ceasing the empress of heaven
The sorceress is a mighty witch with cunning that is brave
and our daughter will have many talents mistress
God I cannot contest mine beloved madame liege Miranda

20th

Prayers of an angel rise up to God, He hears me
God, I have prayed to Thee for but one favor
Ye have heard my heart constantly pleading it
I kneeled down and began to confess and have not ceased
They have desires of grandeur, but their love is not for her
they have other fancies, but I desire mine empress
She seeketh the highness and I her bosoms
She wanteth for blessedness and so I must provide
therefore I must pay homage to my Lord
God, they can be sure that I have waited on Thee
They are assured of Thine work in my life
Faith in God shall bare the fruit of its labors
and I have labored in romance for my lady
I am in waiting for my empress, she can come to me
She is welcome to mine gifts which art love and pleasure
I have many talents but the happiness of mine beloved stands out
She will hear music & be treated to her heart's content of love
I feed on the fluids of her femininity or fret for her foot to kiss
O madame only remember that I love you and your love for me
These art not poems, these art not verses, these are emissions
honestly emitted from longing to be found by her curiosity
Her interest be intrigued at the words she hath heard
spoken by an angel who haunts her
A book is a legacy, it manifests history, It speaks of a mystery
It tells of a time, awakens the mind, and teaches a novelty
I would teach faith in God and love of mine noble family
influencing my people toward majesty
I have spoken to Abraham Moses, Joshua, and David, Elijah
Jesus, Samson, Solomon, Samuel, Isaac, and all the kings
I have spoken to the ghosts of emperor's past for counsel

21st

God, please tell me how to pray. Please, how to serve You best.
What can I say as an author, as a poet, as an artist to be loved
It was severe pain that wrote these standards to her majesty
The pain of wanting when it is most agonizing worse than starvation
I have tried dying and it would not work, and am thus in anguish
for I think my pain shall never be relieved until I have mine empress
This pain it says that God is real & that He hath made me immortal
It tells me that mine wife & I art in heaven & we art its potentates
This pain is both paralyzing and inspiring for it drives me to beg
It is love and I cannot help it, I can only pursue it, It does not leave
God the pain of servitude is more than Ye know be most merciful
Ye cannot have enough mercy Lord, Ye cannot show enough
Thine servant requireth Thine help, in need of Thine sympathy
empathize with me O Lord be with me please answer me my prayer
My faith in Thee is sure God let there be no doubt that I glorify Thee
for I have asked a great blessing of Thee something unheard of
God it is to tell of Thine deft faultlessness and perfection O Lord
Faith will manifest miracles by The All powerful God Infinite
For Yourself God have all of my life and its deliciousness
Savor this life God and be most majestic in it for glory's sake
The empress be purely chaste and innocent as a virgin O Jah
Your potential exceeds the imagination of muses and artists
Even dreamers cannot find the beginning of Your secrets Yahweh
The mysteries of the eternal Creator extend beyond reason or logic
The sciences art not able to calculate You Lord, Ye surpass
statistic
You are a fright to behold for Thine marvelous works terrify my soul
The chariots of Israel and its horses art not as stately nor incredible
as the the armies of the nations of angels and demons sworn to
the great high throne and genii emperor under a sacred oath
They wait on God kneeling at His high tabernacle Jahshua Christ

22nd

Saul hath inquired of a gypsy the council of Samuel
and Elijah was the retort of The Lord to Israel
The people of The New World have built Los Angeles
and Jahshua shall sit upon its most eminent throne
God hath prophesied for the fulfillment of prayers
He shall make the people aware by the children
of His Most Great High Majesty and Magnificence
The faith of Jahshua is notable and unparalleled
He is in constant derision among men because of
their anxiety and need for the assurance of God
Therefore He hath made majesty to be His own glory
Nary shall there be doubt of God's presence
while The Great High Genii answers all wishes
performing all the favors of His subjugation
The congregation hath prayed at the end of the Earth
and Jahshua lives as an angel among the human race
Jahshua is the resident emmanuel forevermore
His spirit is the eternal spirit of spirits that cannot die
The Creator places Himself at the noble pinnacle
He is dignified in the upright tabernacle of majesty
The fathers of Jahshua are all noble and live without vanity
Jahshua's purpose is absolutely for God's reasons
God reveals but a small feat with Jahshua compared to
His inherent ability which reaches the farthest ranges
Lord please be kind and pity this Your servant
Of all of Your lives and spirits God be good to mine
for I have not been rebellious against You Lord
I have not defied Thee in the slightest
but always given Thee mine complete respect & devotion
The Lord is my Lord and there is nothing but Him

23rd

Read the Ecclesiastes the Proverbs and the Psalms
read the gospels and learn their noble wisdom
this is where majesty resides in honest truth
Majesty is the care for Thine people and fellowship
it is the compassion of humility and humanity
we who give hope to the spirit art majesty
we who show love to those in need art beautiful
but the selfish warmongers art wretched on the Earth
We who influence philanthropy have majesty
We art superb for our ability to strengthen and be strong
We stand for support of the survival of sacred life
We appreciate every gift of God with graciousness
Our heart is helpful until it hurts unbearably
We do not heap up our riches but utilize them charitably
Our denizens need their health and nutrition
they need comfort and attendance to live
Majesty is the host that welcomes those in need
The house that opens to everyone and cares for all
The caregiver is most majestic is most pious
I will welcome you in the name of God
and virgins shall wait on You God
Only the most diligent shall be in Thy train
Only the meek shall be allowed Your protection
God this fire that Ye set piques in my veins
it makes me a mighty ferocious beast of a thing
an angel and a demon and a sort of fantasy
O God protect the majesty that mine desires longs for
Make this mine life miraculous in its joy fulfilled
O let me not fail Lord, but succeed in this mine quest
The prayer that I have been inspired with vexes me

24th

This sleep torments me, but faith eases mine worry
God is the difference between mine distress and confidence
Because of the illustrious beauty of mine empress
I should be very afraid for her vulnerable state
but God assures me everyday with His grace and pomp
When I rise I see His face and He calms mine spirit
He whispers soft promises that convince me of His love
thank God that He is loving and caring and not evil
He is a very nurturing God to those who trust His love
He holds all the power and I can only hope to persuade Him
I am exalted to a vertiginous height when I kiss His toe
and striving toward His face I am thought lunatic
Seeking God is not easy but the definition of servitude
We art not ordinary, His devout art a rarity that He cherishes
One can not have too much faith in God but doubt is deadly
It is not faith that torments me but doubt
To endure life on Earth is grueling because of a lack of faith
The standards of majesty art written at God's instruction
for the people to recognize Jahshua as a saint
He is the saint of good attitudes who makes the people joyful
He is all things can do all things as a emperor and genii
Thus he hath rule of everything and allows His mind to manifest
Ye art a dream to God who lives in Jahshua Christ Divine
His life is thus sacred and if he should die only God knows
Jahshua selleth books for her majesty's pleasure
These poems are to marry her majesty in a most royal fashion
O the most noble lady is gracious to her princes and husband
and the princesses can come to us with anything they wish for
They art born great high genii from Jahshua the singular image

25th

Riches to Your devout and dedicated O God to survive
Wealth unto the empire and its denizens O Sire of all Empires
I am only a face to The Lord and He speaks with mine chords
A genii is among you and if ye ask his favor he shall grant it ye
Your hearts content is the blessing of God because He loves us
rule your life with even the slightest majesty and you art gracious
ye stand up for goodness and loving kindness and bravery
valiance is in majesty and righteousness which can be dignified
You who art humble and charitable are the most joyful
he who is loved is cared for and will be remembered well
Therefore be majestic with your posture and look to God for action
be thou dedicated to the Lord and His goodness shall come to you
see that you obey God and study Him and do not forget him
Thank Him as much as possible with bona fide enthusiasm
for He is most spectacular the God all Hosting is
The Lord lives in me to coerce you to believe in Him
He quoth to look at thine spirit and see thine own heart
Look into yourself and know what is good for life
See out into the Creation and set Your heart toward joy
for magnificence is vanity and majesty is worthless
what is of great value is the fulfillment of your own desire
Do as God inspires you then for He hath made thee to fulfill thee
It is by the faith in God that His blessings descend
If we reach for God He will give us of Himself
We will be immersed in God's unlimited plentitude
O God I have reached, I have shown a singular faith
it is greatest knowing the meaning of trust in the Lord
By study of the gospels did this wisdom come about
Look and see how wealthy the great high genii hath become
by His testament to Jesus Christ and The Holy Spirit
The Almighty Father is called the Emperor and Throne Jahshua

26th

Majesty unto the emperor of angels and the cosmos and
His gracious Host The Lord God Almighty Hosanna in the Highest
The tabernacle of the most high is called Jahshua and this is glory
for his God Who calls him Son & Father of Holy Sons & Daughters
What shall I write when I seek majesty prominence and respect
How shall the Lord God reward the steward of His High Empire
The steadfastness of stewards is stellar to see and pleases God
In the presence of majesty we acknowledge his reign
Jahshua reigns over anarchy for God's sake by being all powerful
I went to sleep praying for my empress, I woke up in the same state
I went through the days without ceasing in this prayer
and I begged my God to suit us to each other
I kept my faith in God and I prayed to Him with fervent desperation
because my heart was made with a determination
Now you know that God hath made Jahshua specific to make
a certain statement and testament with His life
The power of God's intent is His glorification
My soul is made for my Lord and my empress and my children
He hath made me to inspire the future to strive with Him
This life is to strengthen the trust in God and this work to prove Him
We say the Almighty hath shown much favor and my day is blessed
As the spirit awakens unto life it looks for meaning
wait on God to guide you and you shall find your fulfillment
this is majesty, when one is most fulfilled
when one is complete and assured
it is the security and sanctimony of faith
what God provides is a reward for our richness
which originates within as an attitude and a confidence
and becomes the noble aura as our faith extends outward
for the betterment of all entities, most especially God

27th

The Majesty of God is His Great High Lord Genii Emperor
Bow to Jahshua and be honored under the scepter of God
His Son is saintliest of all Holy men, His son Jahshua
God answer mine prayer for Thine most loving tender caring mercy
O that Ye cradle Your child as a babe and pamper him with virgins
carry Thine beloved on a cloud Jah promising him her majesty
Mine beloved is The Lord His great angelic courier proclaims
God hath given power to Jahshua in order to be glorified
A champion of the third world shall be crowned king in victory
The high champion serves the cause of God's goodness
The Spirit of Christ is upon Jahshua & the power of Elijah
See the halos of The Great High Angel and His wings
His armor gleams upon the muscle of his flesh like scales
his eyes art ablaze with passion for the cause of The Lord
The nation of His majesty is blessed with magnificence
and highness rises because of the prayers of His servant
to live in the name of God is a great opportunity which I seek
O Lord I stand in the beauty of Thine creation and bask
Ye art most pleasing and delicious is the life I live
in the surreal transports that God manifests in me
An emperor is born a prince of purely noble blood
he rules the country with grace and lives in majesty
God hath made Jahshua His great high imperial lord majesty
for the sake of His own contentment and satisfaction
In gardens hidden by high fences he perches a spirit
there a psalm is played that cannot be retracted
On couches of plush down the king will lay his head
and rare jewels art set about the princess
However the high emperor cannot be deposed
His immortality is most eminent and real
God lives forever in the sole origin the high genii

28th

The wisest of the enlightened seek honor for their prestige
it is the serenity of the spirit and the pride of nobles
honor is the legacy of the respectable advocate
we pursue the welfare of our desolate fellow, we decent ones
the state of the poor is unacceptable to the just
we see the suffering of our race and are impassioned
Our pity forms the foundations of charity so even the lowliest eat
the efforts of the mighty manifest the hope of the meek
we strong art held responsible for the splendor of the nation
We who were blessed with advantage art goodly in humility
A great liberator will be exalted far above the oppressive tyrant
The hero will live more sumptuously in a loving fellowship
than a scoundrel in the cold loneliness of his own spoils
The child that learns charity will live in renown among their peers
They art like kings with loyal servants and great estates to rule
He who controls the capital conceives the charitable action
Therefore the investment in philanthropy will be most rewarding
His work is recognized by its result and thus becomes his majesty
and he will live in the condition that he hath labored for
Ye strive toward providence that toil for the congregation
we uplift the downtrodden by our gracious attitude
when a rich man enters a poor country he becomes a paragon
he will be accepted and venerated by the natives
Give unto those in need for ye art in need of honor
Thy dignity is earned through generosity indeed
and ye shall be recognized by the advancement of thine venture
when the needy rejoice they shall sing of their deliverer
Commit unto the cause of harmony that thy grace be praised
Then when God considers thee, ye be found worthy of peace
The Lord is most worthwhile and will recompense thee rightly
Justify thyself with selflessness, be exalted for goodliness

29th

A standard is a condition to meet a certain aim
I have aimed at majesty I have promised myself to The Lord
Therefore these standards are sacred and Holy for Him
He hath made this text to glorify Himself with beauty
His artist is very beloved to His soul to bless Him so
God hath surely made Himself an avatar to try
His chosen knows all His lusts and how he keeps His peace
The serenity of God is in His meditation which is in His infinite mind
The brain of God surpasseth all brains and knoweth every realm
He surrounds it with His spirit and striveth towards perfection
A standard is like a ritual or a style, it is a type of poem
These are standards and they art standards for royal majesty
Majesty in my country is a great blessing and is hard in my state
Royalty shall make mine majesty It shall be committed to God
The prophet of God upholds His messiah and His sacrifice
The Great High Angel is but a servant of Holy Majesty
Therefore His Holy Bible is His royalty and all His church
and I am a support in His congregation a testament
By royalty I shall testify and this is the standard of majesty
I have reached the foundation for it and am so therefore ruling
over mine own empire of laborers who oversee mine networks
This story is about godly monopolization which is noble
It is in the name of honorable virtue for pedagogical reasons
Jasiah shall read and say he knows my work but shall not
for my work surpasses and continues forever with its commodity
It shall be an heirloom and a treasure that greatly appreciates
He shall be blessed by its extensive popularity as a prince of war
On this day I publish The Charm of Princes these as masterpieces
My message will be pray to God for the wisdom to please Him
and to live with goodness, passion, honor, and respectful humility

30th

I shall go to battle with a fire in my stomach and fury in my heart
wielding large canons dressed in heavy metal armor that flies
and rain fire on the people until the sun goes out forever
and then shall I reside in a mothership which hovers in space
traveling from solar system to solar system in luxury
My farms and oceans are great the people live on my planet
It travels from star to star and galaxy to galaxy
My soldiers wear titanium magnet armor from apple
I shall have a president for my democracy over its population
The mothership, my space station
It will be a earth sized structure with landings for its jaunt ships
Alloy plastic in metal frame on clocklike mechanic nano chips
Mine engineers and technicians work along with the physicists
collaborating with fabricators consulting mechanics
Who are designing a portal and a wormhole
By the year 3000 AD I will have been immortal in flesh a millennia
It is good to be all powerful says The Lord and I have chosen to
reside in my servant as emperor of everything forever
He will be mine designated and I will name him after myself
He will be called Jah and shall be prophesied as The Father
His seed was conceived immaculately and is called messiah
This is His Great High Imperial Magnificence
upholding His Holy Pure Majesty
The Holy Spirit moves throughout for the pleasure of His chosen
God hath blessed himself and made Himself worthy of opulence
He is meant to be richly blessed because of the trials of His soul
God hath been working to be worshipped for His Highness's sake
Jahshua is God forever and none but Himself can revoke it
Glory be to the God of the Great High Angelic Emperor
who hath shown the extent of His The Lord God's mercy